GIRL WAKE UP AND LET HIM SLEEP

By Tricia Simone

Girl Wake Up and Let Him Sleep
Tricia Simone

Library of Congress Cataloguing –in Publication Data is on file at the Library of Congress, Washington, DC
ISBN: 978-0-9815020-7-6 (digital)
ISBN: 978-0-9815020-8-3 (print)

Scripture taken from the New King James Version. Copyright Â© 1982 by Thomas Nelson, Inc. Used by permission. All rights reserved.

GIRL WAKE UP AND LET HIM SLEEP, VOL. 1
By Tricia Simone
Published by The Master's Expressions
Box 841788 Pearland, Texas 77584
www.themastersexpressions.org
Layout & Design by: www.madnessmarketing.net
For longer inclusions contact info@triciasimone.com

TABLE OF CONTENTS

ACKNOWLEDGMENTS

To my mom and dad, thank you for demonstrating and setting the example of a godly marriage. It can be done, and your walk together has given me hope that with God, all things are possible.

Chris & Kimberly Pritchett – Thank you for your support, strong love and obedience. Who knew those late night chats could yield into something so liberating. I'm glad I woke up!

Mrs. Nicole – Thank you for listening, encouraging, and praying me forward. Your friendship is priceless as you pushed me beyond my limits to ensure that I did not get stuck. I will eternally be grateful for you fostering an environment for me to be awake. My 'suddenly' has arrived.

Joey Bismark – If not for you, this book would have a different ending. Your compassion, honest, straight-shooter mentality has kept my feet leveled and grounded. You and your family have been a pillar to me while writing this book. Your feedback and words of wisdom have proven true and I pray others will soon trust the Lord in their situations.

Kundayi Musinami – Thank you for being my coach, friend and brother. Your belief in my story has propelled me into completing this work. I am grateful for your pragmatic, yet tenacious drive as you pushed me to exceed my expectations.

Darnell Tharp – Thank you for allowing me to be me. I am grateful for you being there for not only for me but my family. Your obedience to the Lord, has left an imprint on my soul and for that I thank you.

A special thank you to the following individuals who without their contributions and support this book would not have been written:

Girl wake up and let him sleep

Rhonda Geddis

Midori Henderson

Valinda Vasquez

Jamecia Williams

Tracie Waggoner

Keysha Anderson

Allison Polly

Miranda Luquette

Judy Maldonado

Destiny Lester

Iris Flores

Jade Bismark

Jana L. Early

Kathy McGibbons

Hope Mosby

Patricia Price

Jada Simpson

Babatola Alowuyi

Kayla Tennison

Nadia Sierra

DEDICATION

To all the ladies who have ever fallen head over heels for a Prince Charming. You thought he could walk on water, do no wrong and would meet every requirement you had on your secret check list. Wait, there is a Secret checklist? What is that? Well, we are glad you asked. Here are a few Mr. Perfect checklist items you may or may not have considered. Prince Charming had to:

1. Honor, respect, and love God

2. Be purposeful with integrity and character – etched in confidence (a bit of swag would not hurt)

3. Be kind, nice, and genuinely thoughtful

4. Demonstrate intelligence by being well-spoken on any one of the topics concerning current events/news, business and/or politics

5. Be easy on the eyes ☺

6. Make me laugh. A Kevin Hart type of humor. Not a cute tee – hee- hee laugh, but the kind of laughter that makes your stomach hurt.

7. Respect my parents/family – he may not agree with them, but he will not disrespect them. (refer to bullet 1, being kind)

8. Have Height >5'7 (even though an un-named person is 5'0)

9. Be easy on the eyes (a gentle reminder) ☺

10. Be health conscious and physically fit; toned (Body Builder is not a pre-requisite but it will not be held against him)

11. Have a viable income

The above list maybe overkill, but you should get the idea that a few of you can identify with.

This list was to keep one focused, in line and not get distracted from those who were not of the elect. (Tweet)Irony sets in- as the one who was not perfect (yours truly), sought after and created a list for Mr. Perfect. His perfection would be temporary. It would only exist until he violated the next secret list. The top 10 things he better NOT do!

In reality, it is irrelevant whether your list was written on paper or carried in your heart. This is dedicated to all the single ladies, who are dreamers, wish list makers, honey-do this experts, planners, and controllers in any relationship. There is a new list being created, and this time, it's not for him, but for you. Get ready, because, girl, you're about to wake up!

PROLOGUE

Let Him Sleep (LHS) is more than a few words on a couple of pages. It is an awakening and revelation to what has been available since the beginning of time. It is an inspiration to those situations, circumstances and relationships that have deemed themselves hopeless, impossible, and incomprehensible. The road less traveled can be encountered in increased numbers if a different set of lenses accompanied us on our journeys. Let Him Sleep is the optical Lasik surgery that will reveal a new way to approach and perceive relationships.

In [1]Genesis 2:21 "And the Lord God caused a **deep sleep** to fall on Adam, and <u>he slept</u>..." Adam was clueless, oblivious, and probably snoring. The Lord then, "took one of his ribs and closed up his flesh in its place. (*New King James Version,* Gen. 2:21). Emergency surgery took place. Now, what would have happened to Adam if the procedure God performed had been interrupted? Better yet, had Adam's siesta been tampered with, would Eve even exist?

Ladies, "Let Him Sleep." Who is He? He can be your Bae, Boo, Baby Daddy, and/ or Prince Charming. Do not call, text, email, tweet, engage on Facebook, Instagram (IG), or use any social media to contact him. Absolutely no intermittent dialogue through suggestions or recommendations. There shall be no chit-chats, no

---

[1] *New King James Version, Gen. 2:21*

small talk, no helping a brother out, no nagging, no more reminders of 'I told you so', 'he never listens', or telling him he's no good and lazy. Do nothing but Let Him Sleep. For some of you, I could stop right here, huh? Nope, we've got work to do, and some of us need to wake up. So please continue reading.

Why should you not help him, and wake him up? Because a miracle is taking place within you! Let Him Sleep (LHS) is a journey and excavation of the female finesse, sharpness, and polished eccentricities. This could be a story of a beautify butterfly that simply flew out of her cocoon; however, the reality is the journey began in the larvae stage as a caterpillar. In the end, a new creation emerged, but the details reside within the process. So, wake up and arise ladies! The world awaits all of your glory.

A woman whose focus is solely upon a certain Prince Charming may, at times, put the cart before the horse. For instance, persistence and tenacity help to identify her new victim; oops we mean identify her new mission - under no circumstances are you allowed to let go of Prince Charming! He is open to getting a chance to know her, but in an effort to seal the deal, she introduces elements he's not quite ready for, such as commitment. There are sacred discussions within the female code that are only allowed to remain within sisterly confined quarters. There is absolutely no reason or condition for releasing private details to a person of interest, when a commitment has not been agreed upon. Pre-mature activity only leads up to disaster. For example, on the first date, informing Prince Charming that a certain ring has been selected, along with the location, to host a very significant event (Your wedding) is a clear no-no. Not only will he not be ready for date no.2, but date no.1 has ironically ended rather quickly. He is now scarred from the thought of ever being in any form of commitment. It has happened to the best of us. You were excited and saw clear signs he had potential and was a good friend, so why not talk to your new friend about anything and everything? You were just sharing your heart with hopes of him reciprocating. Sadly, Prince Charming is scared, as he was only trying to get to know you, date you- not marry you. Date no.1 is not the best time to lay out all of your fantasies. Your dreams and aspirations are equivalent to your heart of gold. Do not cast your lovely pearls before someone that has not proven his worth. Wait and see.

Am I saying, on the 1st date, one should not set expectations? Absolutely not, those expectations are critical boundaries, which have to be established early, so both parties are not wasting time. So, instead of erecting healthy constraints by sharing our jewels of wisdom slowly, we vomit our dreams all over someone, who was just in the filtering phase of a possible friendship. What is the filter phase of a relationship? It's the opportunity to discover the best and worst of someone else. This is a two-fold process. While you're searching for Mr. Perfect, he's seeking Mrs. Right. The filter phase is just one aspect of the Dating Stage. Dating is:

- NOT about sex

- NOT about marriage

- ABOUT establishing a good friendship

- ABOUT learning about the other person and YOURSELF

Dating allows you plenty of time to find out more about him. Setting expectations protects your future decisions and properly frames your friendship for success. Think of expectations as your set standards. You're not reading this book to play a game. You want to invest in your future wisely, in all areas of your life, including the relationship arena. You should have a plan of where you will be in 5 years. So, when sharing your expectations, ensure they are also aligned to your life plan. Once you both share each other's expectations, then let's put those words into actions. Let him demonstrate interest consistently and then earn the opportunity to hear your dreams.

Oftentimes, we get excited, anxious, and eager when just a glimpse of potential emerges in someone else. They did not have to even believe in themselves. We'll do that for them, we have enough love to believe for both of us. That is a great trait; however, it should be reserved for someone who stands out and reciprocates openly (without resistance nor our assistance) in displaying their true feelings.

CHAPTER 1:

WAKE UP!

June 2007: To my friend, my lover, my companion and personal confidant. The journey has been an awe-inspiring adventure. Thank you for being you – the only one who puts a smile on my face, makes my heart bubble, the one I have thoughts of kindness, respect, and complete/pure adoration.   May the Lord continue to bless you, may His face shine upon you, and may you be a blessing to many and an enemy to few.

Love Always,

Your help mate, your rib, your soulmate, but most importantly - your friend.

... We interrupt this reading for an emergency broadcast message. The above dedication was so poetic and romantic. It should have been, because ladies, at the time, those were heartfelt words! The reality is the feelings captured in the above were not reciprocated. What happened? Even though the relationship was a challenging, complicated, confusing and rocky, I remained hopeful, confident, and down-right disillusioned. Yet, I did not release him to sleep.

Ladies, read this carefully ... Let Him Sleep (LHS). What exactly does that mean? It translates into 'Leave him alone, give him his space, and do not help to convince him of anything; he does not need your help.' Resist the temptation of walking in the role of being his mother, even if it seems necessary or justified. Playing the mom role is not an option. Panic sets in with a cold sweat, as thoughts rapidly fire off: "OMG if I left him alone, he may never return!" If you gave him his space - what would **you** do? Drama attack manifests, and you are unable to breathe.

If this truly is the case, then you definitely need to consider letting him sleep. If you have gone through any roller coaster emotions over somebody who clearly is in a state of confusion, give him his space and LHS.

Key Messages to Wake-Up:

1. In our quest for looking for Mr. Right, do not negate the fact that YOU have things to work on, individually.

2. There is a dual- purpose for dating: getting a chance to learn about the other party, while learning about yourself in the filtering phase. Understanding your responses, pet peeves, and personal tolerances.

3. Know and understand clearly your expectations, regarding any friendships.

4. Communicate and share those expectations early.

5. Share expectations, not personal fantasies.

---

[2] Designed by Freepik.com

CHAPTER 2:

BEFORE HE SLEPT

Let us take a closer look at Prince Charming by examining his motivations, passions, and areas of focus prior to the deep sleep. From the beginning of creation, Adam was commissioned to tend to the garden. God had already created male and female counterparts in the animal kingdom (dogs, cats, lions etc.) However, the male's task was to take care of everyone and everything, while making sure all was organized in its proper place. He was The Man. His role was defined and detailed; his assignment was purposeful and adventurous. Our Prince Charming, in the beginning, entered a created world of agendas and meetings with sectors of a variety of kingdoms. This is an important concept for females to appreciate. The Man was designed to provide solutions, ensuring his environment, the animals, and the earth were all in order. He was commissioned to subdue and have dominion over the earth.

Any one of our fathers, uncles, brothers, or male cousins may start a casual conversation that will eventually end up in a dialogue,

---

[3] Designed by Freepik.com

regarding what they do. I'm an athlete, I'm a doctor, I handle XYZ Operations, etc. [4]When you listen to a group of ladies speak, you may hear how they felt about a certain topic. It is important for ladies to be understood. For self-expression, we may resort to words that reflect our emotions. Have you ever talked about a problem to a male friend and wanted to be able to express yourself and be heard, and that's it? Somehow or another, the male counterpart may have automatically assumed you needed a solution, when you really only desired that they listen. Now, timing is critical if you really want your man to listen. So, if there is any, and I do mean any, type of ball being thrown or kicked in their view (i.e., basketball, baseball, football, and soccer), I beg of you; don't do it. Don't do what, you ask? Do not interrupt his ritual. Save it for half-time. ☺ Because, if you attempt to break or violate their sacred sports time, you may as well have performed a root canal on him with no anesthetics. However, if you do wait for the right moment, he may end up hearing you with a similitude of sincerity. Your next challenge is his response, [5]because it is nearly impossible for them not to provide a solution. It would be like watching Michael Jordan, standing in his favorite court, with a basketball in his palm – except he is forbidden to do a slam dunk! It's painful for them to not solve a problem. Remember, in the beginning, Adam was a solution provider with a busy schedule to maintain. Visualize the detailed tasks required to tend and keep the famous Garden of Eden. He provided all answers, and if he stopped, jokingly, his efficiency rate may have declined. He numbered the cattle, defined the hierarchical structure of the plant kingdom, and befriended Waldo the canine. Adam's life was his work! So, while Adam pondered his next project, God spiced up the entire program.

---

[4] *Love and Respect: The Love She Most Desires: The Respect He Desperately Needs, Eggerichs, Dr. Emerson*
[5] *(Harvey)Act Like a Lady, Think Like a Man, Steve Harvey ,52*

Key Messages to Wake-Up:

1. Prince Charming is equipped to solve problems and fix things. He is not your BFF (best female friend)

2. Understanding the basic personality traits between male and female will help any current or future relationships.

3. What are your current expectations of Prince Charming? Are they realistic?

4. Establish realistic expectations for your Prince Charming.

CHAPTER 3:

PROGRAM SLEEP, THE UPGRADE

Sleep, the final frontier. These are the voyages of the girl, who woke up from a hazy, foggy slumber. Sleep is the state of having one's motor activity suspended or nearly a complete inactivity of voluntary muscles with partial unconsciousness. It is accompanied by seclusion, concealment, and privacy. When we sleep, neither our family nor our best friends are able to enter our dream world. Sleep was designed as a solo act, requiring no outside influences. This is the posture we ought to release our Prince Charming towards. A good night's sleep. Why? Because the purpose of sleep is to allow the body to reset itself,

---

⁶ Designed by Freepik

while cautiously introducing rejuvenation, restoration, and rest. 'Let Him Sleep' or let him rest, let him be still, let him be restored.

Sleep is an innate part of our makeup. When neglected, it can severely impact and disrupt your physical, mental, and emotional being. We all are wired to allow our bodies to reset, whether we like it or not. Have you ever seen a baby who fights going to sleep? The mother has to orchestrate and attempt to set the right atmosphere, conducive for the baby to feel comfortable to sleep. While, the baby has not developed speech skills, there are clear visible and audible warning signs of sleep deprivation. With no words, the child activates an alarm of siren, which alerts the mother - something is clearly wrong. Sleep is required. In the context of LHS, we are the baby, fighting every opportunity of not releasing Prince Charming to sleep.

Recall how God caused a deep sleep to come on Adam. Not just a normal sleep, but a DEEP sleep to occur. So deep, the Good Book does not outline the meticulous details of Eve's creation. Eve was likely completely clueless as to what had been done around her, in her, and for her divine purpose. All this occurred while, 'you know who' snored on. For as Adam laid in a deep coma, the removal of his rib was used to form Eve's rib cage, lungs, esophagus, intestines, heart, ovaries, womb, appendix, blood, brain, nervous system, neurological system, eyes, teeth, mouth, attitude, snappy responses, humor, mood swings, heightened hormones. God formed all of her, and it was private. Adam nor the paparazzi were allowed to be present during this epic occasion. Let's take a pause, because the beginning of this relationship could not be orchestrated by Adam. He was temporarily unavailable. Adam was not awake for the entrance of Eve. Why would God put Adam to sleep? Perhaps, Adam's slumber helped bypass his pain and ensured the integrity factor remained intact; there would be no data corruption to God's Grand Project, Eve. While Adam was asleep, God was orchestrating His divine plan, the first official marriage. Hidden in the heart of the Father was the one with no physical womb (Adam), who would birth the one with a womb (Eve), and the consummation occurs in verse 22 of Genesis 2, [7]"The Lord God ... brought her to the Man." (*New King James Version,* Gen. 2:22).

Unfortunately, what has happened, in some cases, is some of us did not allow Adam to either wake up on his own, or we would not allow him to sleep. We have been so pre-occupied with Adam that we failed to focus on our own development and presentation. Adam's sleep is not only for him, but the prime opportunity for Eve to find herself and her purpose, uninterrupted.

---

[7] *New King James Version,* Gen. 2:22

Key Messages to Wake-Up:

1. While Eve was being formed, Adam was asleep. There are some things that need to happen on an individual level, before getting to the next step in any relationship.

2. Do not hinder your personal progression by pre-maturely disturbing Adam's quiet time and space.

3. What areas in your life do you need to focus your attention on?

4. By understanding the areas in your life you need to pour into, you will make great progress toward your own personal development.

5. While Eve was being formed, she was in the hands of her Creator. Find quality time to develop your relationship with your Heavenly Father. That is the key relationship to be adequately fostered before continuing forward.

CHAPTER 4:

THE GOD SQUAD (GS)

The fall of mankind is an illustration of how self-will against the kingdom of God is not exactly productive.   Jesus knew the expectations of self-will would need to be re-visited, as he instructed us to pray, "[8]Our Father, who art in heaven. Hallowed by thy name, thy Kingdom come, <u>thy will</u> be done on earth as it is in heaven." (*King James Version,* Matt. 6:8). Even the Lord's Prayer was structured in a way for us to understand whose will should have ultimate precedence.   There have been situations where some have, intentionally or unintentionally, influenced circumstances, because they thought God was late. The bible is laced with scenarios where

---

[8] *Matthew 6: 8(King James Version)*

our fore-mothers embraced the opinion that God was not time conscious and needed some slight intervention.

The God Squad (GS) has a strong presence within the bible. You know who they are - those females, who felt the need to make things happen or help God out. The mother of creation, good ole' Eve, was not only the President of the God Squad, but she also was a faithful supporting member of the elite club of First. While, she was the 2nd human created, she holds the cards for being the first named woman, the first female to partake of the fruit of good and evil, the first to disobey God, and the first mother. Yes, her sphere of influence transcends time, as she is known throughout history for the infamous act of influencing hubby to partake of the forbidden fruit. Eve is not the only participant in the God Squad, for later, we see an honorary member inducted into the membership as well. Sarah, the wife of Abraham, putting her foot down and suggested hubby, Abe, to sleep with her servant, Hagar. That's right, all because the Lord told her she would have a child, but the child did not show up according to Sarah's timetable. However, what she did not know was there was a miracle surrounding the arrival of her son, which was to defy both the constraints of nature and time. At the ripe old age of 91, Sarah become the mother of Isaac. Next, we have Sarah's daughter-in-law, Rebecca, also a member of the God Squad, who not only demonstrated impatience, but also favoritism. Patience has always been a virtue and is almost extinct in today's microwave society. History has shown how the God Squad felt it necessary to try to assist God and execute immediate solutions. Solutions always seem ideal, but we've seen, in some cases, they can turn out to be disasters, rather than resolving the initial issue. Ladies, let the Creator complete the process. When you do not understand the purpose of a thing, you tend to abuse it. For example, when you look at the lifecycle of the butterfly, the process is extremely delicate and complex. When you do not understand the significance of its various stages (larvae or cocoon), one could impede or destroy the emergence of the butterfly.

There exist moments where our choices are not immediately detectible. However, when it does manifest, it may yield favorable results. Sometimes, when we commandeer God's plans with weightless opinions, we have a ship held together with spaghetti instead of an anchor. Eve was created to influence Adam as his partner, his equal, not as his God. Being part of the God Squad can be a good thing; just remember to let him sleep, and let God handle the rest.

Key Messages to Wake-Up:

1. In today's microwave society, the characteristic of patience is crucial for us to maintain successful relationships.

2. The God Squad demonstrated the ability not to TRUST an unseen God, during very public, visible challenges. Despite what you do not see, there still is a God who desires for you to Hope more in Him than in your super abilities.

3. Are you trusting God to handle what you cannot see? Perhaps, start a Prayer Journal/List of situations and circumstances you would like to see God change in you, Prince Charming, and your situation.

CHAPTER 5:

WHY WON'T YOU LET HIM GO TO SLEEP?

There are multiple personality traits which may have hindered you from not allowing your Prince Charming to complete the sleep process. Below are personas that are keeping some of us from letting him sleep. You may or may not identify with any of these, but you may know someone who comes pretty darn close!

[9]**MISS K.I.A (KNOW IT ALL)** – MISS KIA is never, ever wrong. She has to be right at **ALL** times and is not to be opposed. She is argumentative, defensive, and almost always single. Miss KIA does not believe Prince Charming's sleep can be justified. Why is that? Simple, because *she* did not think of it first.

---

[9] designed by Freepik.com

[10]**ME-ME AKA THE CONTOLLER** – Twin sister to the planner, but time is not a driver. The God-given right to make the decision is the driver of this personality, as all decisions are run by the Controller. As a matter of fact, Prince Charming has no say. Selfishness is at the root, as this is not a joint effort. Love should consider the other person's interest; however, there is only one interest to be upheld, the controller. Sleep is not required. The longer the sleep, the more time he has wasted on his indecisiveness. She'll make his decision for him.

[11]**THE PLANNER** – She has a set schedule, agenda/program and is fixed on non-flexibility. She has everything on her calendar: when to get married, have her first child, get sick, get well, etc. Time is the driver for the Planner's actions. Anything that would deviate from the original schedule/plan does not allow for any contingency. The concept of Prince Charming asleep is an inconvenience and will delay her project ... oops ... relationship's progression.

[12]**MISS THIRSTY** – Miss Thirsty can be an extreme personality, who has found a good catch and just can't let him go. She is also known as Desperado, as she has lost her identity. Desperation is defined as a person who is not afraid to get hurt or caught. She will not wait and is obsessed to lasso the prize, Prince Charming. In her opinion, sleep is a disruption to her personal agenda due to the urgency of her desperation.

---

[10] designed by Freepik.com
[11] Image by Shutterstock
[12] *Image by Shutterstock*

[13]**THE AVENGER** – This is not Captain America, but payback time! The Avenger feels Adam does not deserve to sleep! Why? Because Prince Charming has put her through hell, spoken lies, betrayed her; he has been unfaithful, and kept up deceitful antics. He should pay for all the pain he has caused. The avenger will ensure that sleep does not occur.

[14]**THE JUDGE** – The Judge is critical and her self-righteous demeanor will overwhelm Prince Charming. Her ruling is fast & furious – Prince Charming is not good enough, not ambitious enough, and does not work hard enough for her. She does not care if he sleeps, as he was not worthy from the start.

[15] **THE PERFECTIONIST** – Her precision and desire to strive for flawlessness is seen by her establishment of excessive and unrealistically high standards. Similar to the Planner but much more strict. For example, she will have 2.2 children on the 20th of September on a warm, autumn day. Adam has no time to sleep, as he will be too busy in his attempt to reach a goal, which cannot be met.

---

[13] *Image by Shutterstock*

[14] *Image by Shutterstock*

[15] *Image by Shutterstock*

[16]MISS HOLLYWOOD - She is an Image Manager, someone who is focused *only* on the expectation of others. She has ignored the need for Prince Charming to sleep; Miss Hollywood is always worried about the Jones's, or what everybody else will think. Some of you may know her as 'Star Struck' or may be aware of HER second cousin, Cousin Gold Digger.

[17]THE RESCUE RANGER –Her aim is to be free from confinement, force, or danger. She is the savior of the day. The Rescue Ranger believes she can save Prince Charming. She clearly sees what needs to be done, when and with whom. Justification is her fuel as the rescuer has *saved* her mate from possible wrong decisions. Her mission is to save Prince Charming from sleeping. Why? Because there is no need for him to sleep if she is there to save the day.

Have you identified with any of these personality traits? The personalities captured here are not exhaustive and you may very well have another quality that was not mentioned. Explore what that is and why it exists then understanding can abound. There is a common denominator amongst all of the behaviors and it resides within the Fear Factor. Fear, the dark shadow which has immobilized many women from embracing their inner strengths and beauty. It is the culprit and enemy of a healthy future whose goal is to restrain you from making progress. Each of the above personas had demonstrated fear in one form or another.

---

[16] *Image by Shutterstock*

[17] *Image by Shutterstock*

Let Him Sleep is about recognizing and bringing awareness to those things that challenge our relationships. It is not about a transformation into the perfect person. Our traits and behaviors should be owned, embraced, and sometimes adjusted. It should help you realize that you have a choice to awaken from the fog, and to un-employ the fear agent so that he and his cohorts will dissipate.

Let's take a look at how we can begin to let him sleep.

Key Messages to Wake-Up:

1. While some of the listed characteristics are extreme, understand you are not being asked to change, but rather, become aware of what you or your partner has experienced. Understanding why we may not want to let him sleep can lend to a different perspective moving forward.

2. Know whoever is for you, will love you for **all** of you.

3. Fear has breathed doubt and insecurity into scenarios to distract you from the root of the matter, YOU.

4. Rather than focusing solely on Prince Charming, begin to zoom into your inner self. Do you know your purpose? Where will you be in 5yrs? 10yrs?

5. Learning from your past can help shape your future and ensure the same mistakes will not be passed onto Prince Charming.

6. Reflect on current or past relationships. . . Are there any consistent patterns or habits that have led to less than ideal

destinations? Write them down and brainstorm on how you could have handled them differently.

CHAPTER 6:

KEEP CRAZY IN A BOX

[18]

You cannot let anyone sleep without first dealing with self. How do you handle conflicts or circumstances not within your control that may justify a heated response? There are plenty of opportunities to express yourself and not let crazy out of the box. What box are we referring to? You know the invisible four-squared mechanism, where we store our emotions. Well, storage denotes it remains intact. Some of us have unleashed crazy out of its cage! The release process definitely should happen; however, the timing and execution of that release is in question. A posture of control will allow you to have one foot ahead at all times. Sounds ideal, but we all know that is not guaranteed. So, here are a few prioritized options to leverage when you want to read Prince Charming his rights:

---

[18] designed by Freepik.com

1. Wait 24 hours. And do what? Absolutely nothing. Yes, you read that correctly. Wait. Count to 10. One of the hardest things for human beings to do is nothing. Take control of the situation and offer the unexpected reaction of no response. In times past, if you have let crazy out of the box, you are expected to rant, rave, pace the room, yell, etc. Give what is least expected- no reaction. Why? Because you will be in control of you. There are some people, who are entertained by drama. If your mate happens to be someone who embraces drama, then we advise you to have them subscribe to HBO. Riding the emotional roller coaster of crazy for someone else's benefit is not in your best interest. It's inefficient to your emotional energy, and you could recycle all that amp of vitality towards better use, investing in you. Now, if you happen to thrive on drama and not your mate, again, it is still inefficient, but will escalate you towards the collision course of not letting him sleep. Just wait.

2. During your 'do nothing stage', your heart and mind will synchronize while waiting. The heat of the moment will dissipate and reason will enter and center you. You may want to interrogate your Prince Charming and believe he is guilty until proven innocent. This is totally understandable, but crazy is an energy and emotion that can either be fed or starved. Either it will control you, or you control it. Starvation is the state that should be achieved. Never make a decision where your mind and heart are not in synch, because when they are not on one accord, crazy will control you and make you its slave. When you wait for alignment, you will no longer react from a posture of defense and desperation, but you will be centered and in control of you. Not him. That's another book, as we are not aiming to control him, only ourselves.

3. Think about what you would say to the named party and write it in a note. Just do not give it to them. Maybe writing isn't your thing, and you have to hear yourself say it. Then make the phone call- just not to him; instead, call and leave the message on your own voicemail. The point we are trying to make is you need to redirect your energy, since a release of expression has to take place. The caveat in this exercise is you will NOT deliver, nor share it with your Prince Charming. This exercise is meant for you to release privately and express yourself in various methods. Remember, he's asleep, and sharing your insight, at this time, might possibly prematurely wake him up.

4. Keep quiet. Do not tell your girlfriends, best friends, your crew, or buddies. Zip those lips, ladies! Why? Because when you repeat the scenario or situation, you resurrect the entire cycle of emotion all over again, and instead of diffusing something, you have now awakened and fed the beast! This is the exact atmosphere in which crazy will thrive. However, if you have spilled the beans anyway, and your girlfriends, best friends, your crew, or buddies have informed you that your man has possibly tread on forbidden territory - still keep quiet. Believe half of what you see and nothing you hear. Your perception is somebody else's reality. So, to eliminate drama, option 3 may need to be reinforced.

Crazy usually stems from a desire to control a situation you do not truly have control over. Release the unknown future to a known God. Remember, you are the one who is supposed to wake up. So, when the situations get heated, try the above steps to ensure your crazy is not out.

Key Messages to Wake-Up:

1. Everyone has a little crazy bottled inside of us. Crazy just needs to know that it is a slave to you and you only, not vice-versa. Do not allow impulsive emotions dictate your future.

2. If crazy begins to get out of control, then have a plan in place for you to execute. Your future self depends on this.

CHAPTER 7:

DO NOT HIT THE SNOOZE BUTTON

By now, the realization should be set that an inner shift has to take place. We have to be awake and alert. There are some key benefits that support 'Waking Up'.

- Self-Awareness – You have a story that can stand on its own. You are now ready to explore your life dreams and aspirations with a passion and zeal, like never before.

- Confidence Booster - The realization that your worth and personal value is not contingent on the opinion of others, the Kardashians, Entertainment Weekly. It is all within you, and that is absolutely liberating.

- Sphere of Influence- The level of encouragement and impact a sleeping person has vs. an alert, conscious person is not comparable. Being awake provides the ability to inspire others into being a better person when they enter your presence.

How can you be successful within that space? Here are some recommendations that may assist you in 'Waking Up'.

RECOMMENDATIONS:

1. <u>Get a mentor-</u> Find someone you can be fully committed and accountable towards. To some, this may be a mother, grandparent, auntie, or godparent, or older confidante. This should be a voice of reason and neutrality that could speak to your situation, without any bias or gain, yet presents the opportunity for humility and respect to surround you. These voices of wisdom, usually, are older, experienced, and have lived life. Remember to keep these relationships balanced, as some people tend to unintentionally make those sound voices of wisdom their God and negate the scriptures.

2. Again, this may eliminate your girlfriends, crew, or buddies, as they are emotionally connected with you. Pray about the Lord leading the right person(s) to speak into your life, who are objective and have nothing to benefit.

   It may be worth noting who NOT to take advice from:

   a. Someone who has had ***no experience*** in a successful relationship. These individuals do not drink their own Kool-Aid and are usually quick to present themselves as the experts in areas where they refuse to apply past lessons towards their lives. As much as we love 'girl talk', sometimes we self-fulfilling prophesies of destruction by adhering to non-experienced /unsuccessful relational guidance.

    b. Someone **_scarred_** and **_bitter_** from previous relationships. So, while I may have lived life, if I am an angry bird that has not been healed, then I contaminate my advice, as it is flowing from a source that has bitter waters. This removes objectivity from the equation, and being neutral and unbiased are necessary for your growth, healing, and self-development. Simply stated, hurting people hurt people.

3.   The act of washing away old, unsuccessful past relationships, and/or things that hindered progress. Dumping our 'old baggage' into a new relationship is a red flag to any prospect. When people look at you, they should see you are a person, who is focused, confident, and someone on their way to completing their assignment and purpose. This can be achieved by being delivered from Image Management. What is Image Management? When I choose to portray someone else for somebody else, to live according to everyone else's expectation, then I've succumbed to the weed bearing, grass killing "Image Management." This pesticide of resistance shackles and chains its victims to the opinions of others. Learn from the past; don't live in it.

4.   <u>Anoint yourself</u> Dictionary.com defines the word anoint as [19]"to rub or sprinkle on; apply an unguent, ointment, or oily liquid to; to smear with any liquid; to consecrate or make sacred in a ceremony that includes the token applying of oil; to dedicate to the service of God." (anoint)

---

[19] http://dictionary.reference.com/browse/anoint

When something is anointed, it is consecrated and separated for God's service, and anything aligned with God will always have value. Anything worth value is worth investing in, so take the time to invest in yourself. This can start by appreciating your gifts, talents, personality, and little quirks – all of those special areas about YOU. If you do not like yourself, who will?

5. Presentation Matters *"Put on your best garment..."*[20] Placing your best foot forward in presentation is a confidence booster and is a win-win for all parties involved. When you look your best, you feel good, and when you feel good, those around you feel and sense the same thing. You begin to smile and radiate confidence. People are attracted to confidence. It is an invisible beam that draws people in.

6. Reposition yourself *"go down to the threshing floor"* [21](*New King James Version*, Ruth. 3:3). This is a tricky stage, as Ruth was instructed to 'MOVE' and position herself. All I have to do is position myself; how do I do that? By focusing on YOUR future. Where do you see yourself in 10 years? How do you get to that end state? For example, do you see yourself working in the medical field? If so, are there any courses or certifications you need to complete? Put yourself in the right position NOW, just in case Adam does not wake up. By you channeling your energy off of Adam, temporarily, you are putting Adam and the situation in God's hands. Actually, positioning yourself is an act of obedience, as God does not require any assistance from us in what will take place next.

---

[20] *Ruth 3:3 (New King James Version)*
[21] *Ruth 3:3 (New King James Version)*

7. <u>Be still and silent</u> *"but do not make yourself known to the man."*[22]*(New King James Version,* Ruth. 3:3)   Be silent. Remember, silence is golden when someone is sleeping. When we are sleeping peacefully, the last thing we would want is to be awakened sharply, especially without invitation. Babies do not like being awoken when they are resting; we all can attest to grown adults, who may display the same behavior infants do when their sleep is abruptly disturbed. Timing is essential at this phase.   Pre-mature activity of forcing one to awaken can abort unknown blessings in the midst of its development.   Do not try to make something happen when the light is not on you.   Psalms 37:7 "Be still and know that I am God."   No other antics are required.

8. <u>Be patience</u> *"...until he has finished eating and drinking."* [23]*(New King James Version,* Ruth. 3:3) Prior to physically positioning herself, Ruth had to be ok with being single. She was obedient to Naomi's instruction, without having any preconceived 'expectations.' Vet your options and make sure you are ok with either outcome. Whether he wakes up or still slumbers. This positions yourself for a healthy emotional outcome, dictated by yourself, not contingent on someone else's opinion. This also allows the right companion the time he needs to awaken and finish eating and drinking.   The instruction from Naomi was complete, as it involved something that can be a challenge to ALL – PATIENCE. Embracing patience requires a mindset change. You do not need patience waiting on him to finish as much as <u>you</u> need patience to be satisfied with yourself. However, some may still ask, how long will he eat and drink? Asking that question

---

[22] *Ruth 3:3 (New King James Version)*

[23] Ruth 3:3 (New King James Version)

drives us back to the previous chapter, "Why we won't let him go to sleep?"

Key Messages to Wake-Up:

1. Everyone has a little crazy bottled inside of us. However, it has only one Master, You. Crazy just needs to know it is a slave to you and you only, not vice-versa.

2. Do not allow impulsive emotions to dictate your future.

CHAPTER 8:

EVE SLUMBERS NO MORE

History has shown women have effected kingdoms, governments, policies, and families. The sphere of female influence is not bound by economic status, ethnic origins, or geographical settings. Women are a force to be recognized, respected, and appreciated. Our beauty and strength are intricately and simplistically woven by our influence. A mother in a third world country will negotiate and bargain with local vendors to ensure food is available for her children. Influence. As Heads of States, women are in positions of power, overseeing millions of people. Influence. Women are advocates for human dignity, whether or not this is seen by the unwavering commitment of the matriarchs in time. Influence. While you may not always have control over what is presented to you; you do have control over how you respond. Mother Theresa, Helen Keller, Rosa Parks, Malala

Yousafzai, Maya Angelou, and many more have been recorded in history as the Graduate Class of Overcomers. Take hold of your area of influence and contribute to the spheres around you in the short window of time granted to you.

Let Him Sleep is really not about Adam needing his space, but about Eve (a woman) who will not negate her development process. This journey may have shattered your initial life's plan to get married, have children, and live in a house with a white picket fence, but you can rebuild. Time spent worrying over Adam and how to keep him will make you lose sight of who you truly are and can become.

A single woman can be happy and invigorated. Embrace the fact that you have a life purpose, destiny, and future only you can achieve. If you still want to get married, then you have totally understood that Adam's sleep has nothing to do with the destruction of your dreams. Get married; however, appreciate that there is one, who is already enamored with you, in spite of your personality traits. He is more than just Creator, God, but a loving Heavenly Father. "Therefore, behold, I will allure her, and bring her into the wilderness, and speak comfortably unto her." [24](*King James Version,* Hosea 2:14) And get this, God does not require sleep nor slumber.

Wake Up! Invest in you, develop your skill set, and identify your strengths and weaknesses. Break free today of the fears, lies, and false pretenses to embrace the future and the bright new day and opportunity to trust your God.

---

[24] *(King James Version, Hosea 2:14)*

ABOUT THE AUTHOR

Tricia Simone, Life Strategist and Self-Esteem Activist is the author of "Girl, Wake Up and Let Him Sleep" and "A Pocket Guide: To My Life Resume." She is a decidedly intense, fiery, and passionate spirit who aims to ignite discussion, invoke ideas and challenge her audiences to explore life's hidden paradigms. Tricia has had the privilege traveling the world as a public speaker and helps people obtain awareness and provides a strategy as it relates to their strengths, patterns and possibilities. This strategy empowers others to make confident decisions which moves them forward to the future they desire.

Born in East Coast Brooklyn, New York of Jamaican parentage and raised in the deep south of Houston, Texas. Tricia Simone views various complex life issues through a unique and diverse lens. She is well known for her very unorthodox but practical and effective method to finding solutions and empowering people at life's crossroad. Audiences can expect to be educated, activated and energized to find the leader in themselves.

Revolutionize your future, by understanding your past!

www.TriciaSimone.com

Index

1. Genesis 2: 21 (New King James Version)

2. designed by Freepik.com

3. designed by Freepik.com

4. Eggerichs, Dr. Emerson. *The Love She Most Desires: The Respect He Desperately Needs*. Nashville: Yates & Yates, LLP, Attorneys and Literary Agents, 1984. Digital.

5. Harvey, Steve. *Act Like a Lady, Think Like a Man*. New York: Harper Collings Publishers, 2009. Print

6. designed by Freepik.com

7. designed by Freepik.com

8. Genesis 2: 18 (New King James Version)

9. Genesis 1: 27,28 (King James Version)

10. Matthew 6: 8(King James Version)

11. designed by Freepik.com

12. designed by Freepik.com

13. designed by Freepik.com

14. Ruth 3:3 (New King James Version)

15. http://dictionary.reference.com/browse/anoint

16. Genesis (New King James Version) 18:14

17. Hosea (King James Version) 2:14

www.ingramcontent.com/pod-product-compliance
Lightning Source LLC
Chambersburg PA
CBHW070110070426
42448CB00038B/2500